The Wright Words

Stories of Inspiration
from the Lives of
Orville and Wilbur Wright

by Kirk A. Haas

The Wright Words, Stories of Inspiration from the lives of Orville and Wilbur Wright.

ISBN-13: 978-1718833036
ISBN-10: 1718833032
BISAC: Education / Decision Making & Problem Solving

Forward

Orville and Wilbur Wright's coin flip at Kill Devil Hills, deciding who would pilot that first historic flight over the sandy Atlantic beach, was by no means the beginning of their aviation odyssey. It actually had it's true genesis in hundreds of dinner table debates, deep discussions, and family disputations, each sharing their ideas with the other, trimming and refining their postulates and positions until resolution replaced wonder.

This fact was largely unknown to me until my friend and co-worker, Kirk Haas, began sharing his vast knowledge of the Wrights and their inspirational techniques of problem solving, brainstorming and deductive thought. Kirk has an obvious and infectious passion for the Wrights, their accomplishments, and their ability to apply reason and process to any conflict, be it aeronautical, social, or personal. That passion reveals itself in The Wright Words, a collection of stories showcasing the famed Wright analytical thought, and yet each with a heartbeat, a human inspirational touch from lessons learned.

Inspirational stories give us more than motivation; they give us hope. The belief we can see a bit of ourselves in each of these stories, the idea that reason and intellect can conquer conflict, all coupled with Kirk's encompassing knowledge of the Wrights and their history, create stories that not only make you feel good, but make you *do* good.

History without stories is a recitation of forgettable facts. Stories without lessons are entertaining, but do not inspire. Kirk has managed to deliver all of this to us in these stories. And we didn't even have to win a coin flip.

Paul G. Labadie
Syndicated columnist

Preface

"The old cat is dead."[1] - Orville Wright, April 1881

These are the words that end the earliest found communication from either of the Wright brothers. It was on a postcard sent to their father, an itinerate minister. Orville was nine years old.

In his book *Miracle at Kitty Hawk, The Letters of Wilbur and Orville Wright,* author Fred C. Kelly has compiled letters written by or to the Wright brothers to tell their incredible journey of discovery in aviation. I have taken quotes found in those letters and from other sources, to share moments of inspiration that we all can use in our lives. Each of us is unique and will find our own stories within these pages.

My hope is that through my interpretation of these stories you, the reader, can find a peaceful moment to reflect on the stories of the Wrights and find a little inspiration.

Thank you first to my wife and editor Valerie, always my inspiration; my two boys, Ian and Cole; Pat Monosky, Dale Whitford and Lawrence Hardy for their encouragement and finally to my friend Paul Labadie who convinced me this was a good idea.

- Kirk A. Haas

[1] *Miracle at Kitty Hawk,* F. Kelly

Contents

Introduction

What follows in these pages are a collection of short essays in which I share the stories of Wilbur, Orville, and Katharine Wright. My essays are written to share inspirational takes on things the Wrights have said or done in their lives.

In 2007, I was hired to present the Wright family stories for The Henry Ford Museum and Greenfield Village, in Dearborn, Michigan. Since then I have spent my spare time studying those stories. I continue to read source material including the many biographies available, including-but not limited to-those listed in this work. The technical aspects of flight are not my forte. I am not an expert on flight, or the many innovations of air flight since the sale of the Wright Company in 1915, when Orville walked away from the manufacture and sale of Wright airplanes.

The area of the Wright family stories on which I have focused my work is that of the people involved in their lives and how they helped Wilbur, Orville, and their sister Katharine live lives of inspiration and innovation.

Through my interaction with the visitors of Greenfield Village, where I work in the Wright Cycle Shop and the Wright Family Home weekly from mid April through November each season, I have come to understand that there is a level of understanding and misunderstanding that the general public has of the stories of the Wright Family. I hope to clarify some of the misconceptions and open a few paths to understanding the adventure the Wrights took through their lives.

I hope to continue my journey with the Wright Family through the remaining years of my life and will continue to learn more and share what I learn. I hope that the stories of the Wrights will inspire you as they have inspired me; to learn, to be better than you were yesterday and to share with the world about you, that which you find.

Thank you for taking a few moments of your day to read my work. I hope it helps you as much as it helps me.

Source Material

With each essay a list of reading material follows. These are the source materials that I have used to find the information used in the essay. Only direct quotes will be cited. The ideas stated can be found through these materials but they are presented in my words with my take on them. My work is factually based but should not be taken as source material for your own work. Please take the time to do your own research. I hope you will find your research as enjoyable as I have found my own.

The Wright Words

Scrapping

"If a man is in too big a hurry to give up an error he is liable to give up some truth with it, and in accepting the arguments of the other man he is sure to get some error with it. I like to sift all the truth out before I give up an error." - Wilbur Wright, 1903[1]

***

As young boys, Wilbur and Orville Wright argued just as any set of siblings are want to do. This is how we learn to communicate and how we learn what works in defending a point of opinion. Facts are facts, but any set of facts can be presented to rationalize any point of view.

Young Will and Orv used what they called 'scrapping' to figure out problems. These problems might range from who gets to play with a toy first to who has to do the dishes that night. For them, scrapping was fun. Scrapping allowed a heated conversation to settle down and eventually to solve the issue at hand.

Scrapping was taught to them by their father, Milton. Milton Wright was a minister who traveled, covering territories west of the Mississippi River. Reverend Wright assisted in the teachings and running of the United Brethren Churches under his care. Rev. Wright would collect interesting toys and books for the boys to stimulate their imaginations and broaden their knowledge.

On occasion he would bring home books on topics that he did not agree with. He encouraged knowledge for its own sake, even if he did not agree. He wanted his children to understand what others believed, but he also wanted his children to know that you do not have to believe every thing you read.

One of the greatest lessons he taught his children was the art of respectful disagreement through the skill of scrapping over ideas. He would stop the boys in the middle of a heated argument and make them switch sides in the argument, continuing the argument from the other person's point of view.

Here comes the kicker: He would make them finish the argument from that other view point without returning to their original. You could not give up to win and you could not sabotage the other opinion. You had to try to win. But you had to try to win from a point of view that you originally thought was wrong.

The lesson learned through scrapping was that every point of view has merit. There is always something good in an idea. Otherwise, the other person would not have thought of it in the first place. Milton Wright believed that if you could find something good in an idea that you did not agree with, you could gather together only the good parts of both views and end the argument faster by respecting other points of view. By putting forth an honest effort to find the good in all ideas, you were showing respect and a determination to resolve the issue at hand.

The Wright brothers used this form of discussion called scrapping to solve many of the misunderstood problems of human flight. They practiced this well into their adult life.

Their employee, Charlie Taylor, told the story that one day the boys were having a heated argument in the back of their cycle shop and stormed out early, heading home for the evening. Charlie claimed that Wilbur came into work early the next morning stating that it was inappropriate of the two boys to argue so heatedly in front of Charlie and apologized for that. He added that he decided that he was going to do it Orville's way instead. Orville arrived shortly after that, pulling Charlie aside to apologize for the argument and stating that they would be doing it Wilbur's way. Charlie told them both that they needed to scrap again as they had gone home and switched sides, just as their father had taught them when they were young boys.

They were so good at scrapping that they had gone home and successfully found the merit in the opposite point of view. Milton had taught them well.

***

[1]*Miracle at Kitty Hawk*, F. Kelly
The Bishop's Boys, Dr. Tom Crouch
The Wright Brothers, A Biography, F. Kelly
Wilbur and Orville: A Biography, F. Howard
*"My Story of the Wright Brothers, as told to
  Robert S. Ball." Collier's Weekly,
  Dec. 25, 1948*, C. Taylor

The Wright Words

16

A Wish to Learn

"If you are looking for perfect safety, you will do well to sit on a fence and watch the birds; but if you really wish to learn, you must mount a machine and become acquainted with its tricks by actual trial."
-Wilbur Wright 1901[1]

***

Many of us lament the problems of today and the lack of solutions being implemented by our leaders. We drudge along with our lives with what we believe are the obvious solutions to the troubles of our day to day lives without taking action to fix them. We believe that someone else will find the solutions and with enough will, take care of them for us. Then we continue on with our lives, continuing to lament.

The Wright brothers stepped into the problem of human flight not as a fix for transportation, to create war machines, or any of the many uses of today's aviation. They had a recreational interest.

They had a bicycle shop that, by 1898, had enjoyed five years of financial success. The bicycle business, however, is a seasonal business with manufacturing in the winter, sales in the spring, and repair in the summer months. There was a bit of down time in the fall and they wanted something to do to fill that time.

Gliding was an experimental activity written about in many magazines and papers. Those papers discussed the many aviation pioneers active since Sir George

Cayley, in 1853, first lifted a man on a wing, utilizing Bernoulli's principles discovered 110 years before.

Wilbur and Orville saw gliding as an activity to fill the days of autumn. In their reading they discovered that all of those pioneers were hitting the same proverbial brick wall of balance and sustained control.

The Wrights knew that if they could solve the brick wall, all they had then to do was apply what all those pioneers had already solved. So that is what they did. They studied birds. They studied balancing a bike. They learned a bird twists its wings in opposite directions to cause lift on only one side at a time. They learned that you shift your hips on a bike and then lean into the turn.

Then they built a glider and got on it. They suffered through more than one hundred rough landings that first year. They learned as they went. They made improvements every year for four years and four machines. They flew their gliders thousands of times. They took risks. They stayed focused on safety but never avoided climbing on those machines. They understood you can learn only so much from watching from afar. At some point you have to climb on and try.

When we look at the world around us, learning from afar, our solutions are only as good as the discoveries made by those few who have climbed on and tried. Most fail; even more never try. But the solutions found, the solutions we implement, are there because of the few who take action. You have to be willing to fail, willing to try, and willing to do the hard work.

Trying is not an invention of the Wright Brothers. Taking action is not a gift from the Wrights. Trying and taking action are a given, recognized by Wilbur and Orville, which they implemented to solve what was thought to be impossible: The problem of human flight.

***

Miracle at Kitty Hawk, F. Kelly
The Bishop's Boys, Dr. Tom Crouch
The Wright Brothers, A Biography, F. Kelly
Wilbur and Orville: A Biography, F. Howard
[1] *"Some Aeronautical Experiments"* W. Wright

Special Quality

"Very often what you take for some special quality of mind is merely facility arising from constant practice."
- Wilbur Wright, 1903[1]

***

Kill Devil Hills, North Carolina was a mile deep, five-mile wide sand dune with a series of hills. Off these hills Wilbur and Orville Wright would float in the air on gliders they constructed back in a workshop in Dayton, Ohio. They would construct the parts in their Dayton bike shop and crate them for shipment to Kitty Hawk, NC. They would have them carried four miles south to a shed they constructed in the middle of the Kill Devil Hills' sands.

This process of constructing, shipping and assembly would cover a four to six month period, performed each year from 1900 through 1902, culminating in a few weeks to a month of gliding practice. Returning home with the data collected and the notes from their experiments, they would analyze the results and prepare for the next year's visit.

Self taught through reading and trial in their home environs, the Wrights learned how to build a flying machine unlike any other that had existed before them. Perhaps the most important aspect of this is not the discovery and creation, but the practice they did on these machines. Wilbur knew that what made a machine successful was the ability to use the machine in actual flight.

In order to learn how to ride a bike you have to climb on and use the bike. Very often it takes many rides to get the hang of it and many more to become proficient. This would be true with a flying machine, Wilbur thought and, therefore, this was the plan: To take the machine to a place where they could climb on and practice flying.

In those first two years, 1900 and 1901, by testing of machines and through climbing on them, they continually improved the efficiency of the machine itself. After a series of wind tunnel tests in 1901, the Wright brothers built a glider that surpassed all gliders built by the many pioneers that preceded them. The 1902 glider was the best made to that date. But something else was needed. They had to learn how to be the best pilots that had ever flown.

Each year they performed hundreds to thousands of trials. Most attempts suffered rough landings with occasional broken parts to repair or replace, not to mention the mouthfuls of sand and the bruised body parts. But this never stopped them from climbing on and flying the few seconds that each flight would last.

Both boys understood that repetition helped riding a bike become second nature, and a process that ingrained muscle memory so much that you forgot that you were doing it. In this process of discovery, Wilbur asked his bike riding friends to explain to him *how* they balanced their bicycles. Very few could answer and most got it wrong. But they all could *do* it without difficulty. This meant that they had forgotten how because they no longer needed to *think* about it. It was second nature to them now. This is what was necessary to become a proficient pilot.

The "special quality of mind" of a successful pilot was just a proficiency acquired through practice—lots and lots of practice. The boys knew this.

***

[1]*Miracle at Kitty Hawk*, F. Kelly
The Bishop's Boys, Dr. Tom Crouch
The Wright Brothers, A Biography, F. Kelly
Wilbur and Orville: A Biography, F. Howard

Making Assumptions of Truth

"You doubtless will make some mistakes, just as we do, and just as everybody else does, but if we all worked on the assumption that what is accepted as true is really true, there would be little hope of advance..."
- Orville Wright, 1903[1]

***

Throughout the work of the Wright brothers in their endeavors to fly, they were continually dealing with truths that other aviators had and continued to accept as true. As Wilbur discovers over and over again, these are false assumptions. From the middle 1890's through the turn of the century, aviators were building gliders based on data compiled by Otto Lilienthal, explaining lift and the shape of wings. When the Wright's tried these same ideas, their success was limited.

Many of the other aviators questioned their own work as flawed when success did not achieve what Lilienthal's data suggested it should. Even the Wrights had second thoughts about their own work. But Wilbur and Orville questioned not only their own work but also questioned Lilienthal's data.

This was a unique approach. A simple test and the crude results of that test led to another series of serious tests, even going as far as to create a wind tunnel to test wing shapes and lift. After weeks of meticulous testing of over 200 shapes, the Wright brothers realized that the assumption that Lilienthal and his data where correct was the true flaw.

The flaw in Lilienthal's formula for lift and the shape of the wing was slight, but made a big difference in the Wright brothers' success. The next glider, which included the new data, was a tremendous success for the Wrights. The new data would lead to the first successful airplane the following year.

Had Wilbur and Orville carried on working only with data compiled by Lilienthal and his peers, the gliders made by the boys may not have succeeded and may have frustrated the Wright's out of the business of flight. They may have not advanced the art of human flight. But they approached the problem from a different path. A path of questioning and not a path of accepting.

It is a typical path to take the information gathered before and to build on that information. We build on what has gone before. But if we fail to question that information and assume the accuracy of it, we abandon a tool necessary for success. The ability to look at data and ideas and dig deeper into how that information was gained, and how it was used in further experimentation, is an important tool that perhaps was overlooked by aviators before the Wright brothers.

Through thoughtful investigation and questioning of accumulated data, the Wrights were able to make discoveries that other experimenters had simply taken for granted. The assumptions that the existing information was accurate held back pioneers for decades before the Wrights. Lessons learned as young boys of an open-minded minister father, taught them not to believe everything they read.

This simple understanding that what you read may have flaws and should not be blindly followed, can be linked to the Wright's final success of human flight.

***

[1]*Miracle at Kitty Hawk*, F. Kelly
The Bishop's Boys, Dr. Tom Crouch
The Wright Brothers, A Biography, F. Kelly
Wilbur and Orville: A Biography, F. Howard

Secrets Preserved

"Isn't it astonishing that all these secrets have been preserved for so many years just so that we could discover them!" - Orville Wright, 1903[1]

***

Fifty years before the Wright brothers flew in 1903, Sir George Cayley lifted a man on a glider wing he had made. This is considered the beginning of human flight. In the fifty years that followed, many engineers, scientists and interested pioneers attempted to fly. The level of success they achieved varied from getting lift and thrust on powered machines, successful gliding for moments at a time covering various distances, to complete failure and, many times, the death of the pilot.

The information compiled is shared through magazine articles, books written and speeches given. It was happening in Europe, America, India, Australia and New Zealand. It was done for fun, it was done for hopes of profit, but it was also done with the knowledge of the others that had gone before. Everyone who achieved a level of what could be called success shared the little knowledge they gleaned. Some held their methods or information back until their success was achieved.

Octave Chanute was an engineer bridge builder out of Kansas but based in Chicago, IL. At the turn of the century he gave up on his attempts to fly, having experimented for years. Knowing that he was not going to figure this out himself, he took it upon himself to be a sort of clearing house of knowledge of the information in human flight. Knowing he would not fly, he wanted to help the others in their attempts.

Octave would become Wilbur's friend and act as mentor to the Wrights. Sometimes his help would move the boys forward and many times it would be simply a friendly conversation and nothing more. For Chanute, what the Wrights were achieving was important information that needed to be shared. Wilbur found this unacceptable as they were getting close to final success and wanted the opportunity to patent their discoveries.

In a letter written to George Spratt, a friend of the Wrights (introduced to them by Chanute, who had spent some time with the boys at their camp at Kill Devil Hills, NC), Orville shared a discovery they had just realized. His amazement was not the achievement itself, but the fact that it was a discovery that had been sitting in front of all those innovators for decades. A secret that had eluded them, which the Wrights discovered.

Orville was amazed and felt blessed that it had remained a secret for so long. Almost as if it was being held out of the reach of the other innovators just so the Wrights could discover it. It was as if there was a reason that Wilbur and Orville would eventually become the inventors of the airplane.

Chanute had made it his life's mission to share the knowledge of aviation experimentation, even to the point of convincing Wilbur to stand before a room of engineers and share what they had discovered up until and through the 1901 season of tests. Yet it was two years later that final success was achieved. Chanute and the many other aviation pioneers would continue to struggle through that time without success. It was as if the aviation gods wanted Wilbur and Orville to be the ones to achieve.

The Wright brothers knew that they were the best gliders with the most efficient machine. By the end of the 1902 season, they knew that they would achieve flight. What humbled them was the amazement that no one before them had figured out *how*, when the answers had been there all that time.

***

[1]*Miracle at Kitty Hawk*, F. Kelly
The Bishop's Boys, Dr. Tom Crouch
The Wright Brothers, A Biography, F. Kelly
Wilbur and Orville: A Biography, F. Howard

In the Beginning…

"I am an enthusiast…I wish to avail myself of all that is already known and then if possible add my mite to help on the future worker who will attain final success." - Wilbur Wright, 1899[1]

***

Looking at the world about you, you will eventually see something that could be done better. You come up with the obvious idea that will solve the problem, whatever that problem would happen to be. For most of us that is as far as it will ever go. You will not take action; you may not even remember the problem you gave your thoughts to by the time you get home. Most of us will never take action.

Solving the problems of the world around us is not simple. If it were, there would be very few problems left to solve. The problems in our world are difficult to solve because it takes hard work and dedication.

In 1896 Wilbur was reading about early pioneers of human flight and their attempts to solve the problem of flight. It sparked an interest but there would be more to read.

Magazines such as Scientific American would tell of Otto Lilienthal, Percy Pilcher, and other prominent scientists and engineers such as Octave Chanute and Professor Samuel P. Langley, who was the director of the Smithsonian Institute. The idea of human flight will be given legitimacy by Englishman Sir George

Cayley in 1853, when his glider lifted a man in the air for the first time in our history.

After exhausting all that he could find in his visits to the local Dayton library, Wilbur needed to know more if he was to get anywhere in his desire to fly.

When we approach a problem that we are passionate about, we desire to know as much as we can. We need to learn what is already discovered so that we don't spin our wheels repeating what has gone before.

Wilbur's desire to know sent him to many sources, magazines, a library and finally the Smithsonian Institute with the letter quoted above. It was the information received from the Smithsonian that was useful and substantial. This is why we historians have identified this letter as the beginning of the Wright's involvement.

It would take Wilbur and Orville four years to design, build and fly the first airplane. Four years of study, theory, and trial. But it started with reading and the study of what was already known. Building on the work that had been done before. Standing on the shoulders of the pioneers who had worked so hard and shared what they had learned, so that they might "help on the future worker" as Wilbur stated in his letter.

Not all discoveries, innovations or invention happens as fast as four years. Especially when it began fifty years before with a man cutting a bird's wing in cross section to learn how it flies. But the Wright brothers were able to accomplish that feat, perhaps because they knew that the pioneers who traveled that road before where not fools or cranks.

Wilbur wrote later that it was the great scientist Samuel Langley's belief in human flight that gave Wilbur faith that it was possible. What you do is important to your success. But equally important is believing that those that went before you believed as much as you, that what you were doing was important and possible.

It is not only the work that goes before you but the faith in your ideas that really matters. A shared faith with others is perhaps the most important.

***

[1]*Miracle at Kitty Hawk*, F. Kelly
The Bishop's Boys, Dr. Tom Crouch
The Wright Brothers, *A Biography*, F. Kelly
Wilbur and Orville: A Biography, F. Howard

Not Sufficiently Accurate

"[Lilienthal's] tables of pressures and resistances of arched airplane surfaces were the results of years of experiment and were the best in existence, yet they were not sufficiently accurate to enable anyone to construct a machine with full assurance that it would give exactly the expected results." - Wilbur Wright, 1912[1]

***

For six years Otto Lilienthal, a German aviation pioneer, experimented with flight. He was considered the preeminent aviator with his gliding and his table of data, helping others with the shape of their wings. The many experimenters in flight throughout the world were following Lilienthal and his flights, in the magazines of the times. They were making gliders based on Lilienthal's gliders and formulas. They were achieving enough success to believe that they were successful, but they were all hitting a preverbal brick wall, balance.

Lilienthal's method of balance was to shift the weight hanging low under his wings; he would shift his legs and lower body left to right. The result was the lift of one wing would rise as the other dropped. It was an effective method but had its limits. It would be this inability to shift his weight far enough to stall the swift lifting caused by a gust of wind of one side of his machine which led to his death. The result was a fall, breaking Lilienthal's back. He passed away the next day. His last words were "Sacrifices must be made."[2]

With the stumbles of 1901, Wilbur questioned whether flight was possible after all. Lilienthal's tables did not give the results that should have occurred. Many aviators were experiencing the failures similar to the Wrights' and questioned what they were doing different from Lilienthal. Wilbur and Orville reconsidered their work and concluded that they were failing to achieve adequate lift, not because of their own work but because Lilienthal's work was flawed. This was a departure from the other aviation pioneers.

Wilbur was invited to give a talk to the Western Society of Engineers at a meeting in Chicago, in September of that year, and discussed with Orville the idea of telling them that Lilienthal's data was flawed. Orville did not think it wise until they had proved it. Wilbur suggested it at the meeting but did not go into detail. It was after his return to Dayton that the boys began their search for proof.

After some success with a crude devise on the handlebars of a moving bicycle they built a wind tunnel and meticulously tested about 200 shapes of wings at multiple angles. The data collected in this manner gave them enough proof to not only believe that Lilienthal was, in fact wrong, but in the process the Wrights had discovered the correct shape. We are still using this shape in today's airplanes.

The quote at the beginning of this essay was written by Wilbur for the Aero Club of America a few days before his fatal illness. It is perhaps his last published work.

Wilbur and his brother Orville are unique in aviation history. They invented the airplane in their workshop in Dayton and perfected the art of flying with their efforts at Kill Devil Hills in North Carolina and over Huffman Prairie outside of Dayton, Ohio. But perhaps their greatest contribution was the willingness to question the accuracy of the accepted work of the best aviator to that date, along with a willingness to do the work necessary to prove their own theories of flight.

***

[1]*Miracle at Kitty Hawk*, F. Kelly
The Bishop's Boys, Dr. Tom Crouch
The Wright Brothers, A Biography, F. Kelly
[2]*Wilbur and Orville: A Biography*, F. Howard

Kate's Romance

"It was natural enough for me to be tender with you....I did know what to do for once." - Katharine Wright 1925[1]

***

In July 1889, Susan Wright, mother of five and wife of an itinerate minister, passed away at home in her bedroom in Dayton, Ohio. It was devastating to the Wright family, but especially to young Katharine, who was about to enter high school. At that time in our history, it was expected that the woman of the house would be responsible for most, if not all, of the domestic chores. Katharine would be expected to take this on at the age of fifteen.

Kate, as she was known then, would juggle school work and those domestic chores throughout her high school years. Her social life would be limited by these duties. High school was the time when social activities would teach young adults those skills needed to find their spouse and then start a new family. Kate's father had needs in addition to the domestic chores which his wife took care of. Correspondences of a traveling minister were crucial to his job and this extra work fell to young Katharine.

Because of the burden that befell Kate, she was limited in her outside romantic opportunities. Her father understood that his needs came first and this would prevent Kate from achieving a relationship and her own family. His concern was that after his own passing

Kate would be on her own without financial support. Her father went against the norm and sent her to college in hopes that she would graduate and find a good job. He sent her to Oberlin College.

Oberlin was one of our nation's few colleges that allowed women to study and graduate and it was one of the first to allow students to study in classes filled with both men and women.

Katharine, as she would be called going forward, lived in a women's boarding house on campus, which was used by select male students to take meals. One of these young men became her math tutor as she struggled in that subject. His name was Harry Haskel and he was a wiz at mathematics. He also came to be interested in Katharine in a romantic way. But having missed his cues, she did not respond. This he interpreted as disinterest in him.

Harry moved on, as she did. He would become involved with a roommate of Katharine's named Isabel. Harry and Isabel would marry and start a family in Kansas City. Katharine would stumble through a relationship with a young sports star at Oberlin named Arthur Cunningham. That would not work out. Katharine would graduate without a relationship other than the ones she formed with her fellow roommates, Agnes, Margaret, Kate, and Harriet. Those relationships would stay with her for the remainder of her life.

It would be ten years later that Harry and Katharine would meet again. This would happen in Washington

DC, at a demonstration of the Wright airplane given by her brother Orville. Harry would be there as a reporter for the Kansas City Star newspaper. Harry and Katharine would begin to correspond through letters for many years to come as college friends did and still do.

In September 1923, Harry would lose Isabel to cancer and would be heart broken. Katharine's letters of consolation would spark a relationship with Harry that would grow into one of romance and, eventually, love. They would be married on November 20, 1926, in the home of friends, on Oberlin's campus where Katharine and Harry first met.

After a life full of adventure with her brothers and a life of commitment to her family, Katharine would know romantic love with a man she met in college. Her father sent her to Oberlin to earn a degree in order to take care of herself after his passing. There was so much more that she gained at Oberlin. She met the man she would fall in love with and marry. Her father did well.

**

[1]*The Wright Sister,* R. Maurer
The Bishop's Boys, T. Crouch

Mentor and Friend

"For some years I have been afflicted with the belief that flight is possible to man. My disease has increased in severity and I feel that it will soon cost me an increased amount of money if not my life."
- Wilbur Wright, 1900[1]

***

Octave Chanute was an accomplished engineer based in Chicago, IL, who had devoted much of his later life to the investigation of aviation. The trussing methods used in his bridge designs were incorporated into his early bi-wing design of gliders. He was not successful in achieving flight, but he believed that final success would be achieved by an association of pioneers working together, sharing ideas, and discoveries.

Chanute took it upon himself to be a leader in the sharing of aviation information. His book, *Progress in Flying Machines,* was instrumental in disseminating knowledge to the many aviators of his time. Wilbur was one of them.

The above quote is the first sentence in Wilbur's first letter to Octave. In his letter, Wilbur asks for information on a suitable location to practice flying. Octave sends him not to Chicago, where Wilbur thought preferable, but instead to the east coast where the winds of the Atlantic Ocean were steady. This would direct Wilbur to their eventual proverbial second home outside Kitty Hawk, North Carolina. The Wright's would visit there four years straight for weeks at a time, culminating in the first flights in December of 1903, at Kill Devil Hills, four miles south of Kitty Hawk.

The relationship built between Chanute and Wilbur would last until Chanute passed in 1906. At times the letter exchange would become contentious but, for the most part, it would be a friendly exchange of ideas in helpful companionship.

Chanute visited the Wrights multiple times. Once to Kill Devil Hills in 1901 to witness their flying experiments. It was on this visit outside of Kitty Hawk that he realized that the boys were very close, and certainly further along, than any other aviator to date. Chanute would ask Wilbur to speak in Chicago later that year to the Western Society of Engineers to discuss the Wright's experiments. A reluctant Wilbur would deliver, in September of that year, a pivotal speech on the experiments they had conducted up until that moment. That speech would be published in aviation magazines in many different languages the following year.

Having someone to bounce ideas off and to steer the Wrights in their journey would benefit the boys greatly. Wilbur would question Chanute's direct involvement in later years, but would acknowledge that his letters were a valuable aspect of success in the end.

Chanute's desire to share the knowledge of aviation experimentation became a problem for Wilbur and Orville when Chanute reveals too much information on what the Wright brothers had discovered and even credits himself as assisting the Wrights in one publication. The Wright's had submitted a patent covering the control mechanism of their glider in March 1903, which they did not receive approval for until May 1906. To reveal the technology covered in that patent could prevent the Wrights from royalty payments going forward.

Wilbur and Octave would make peace through an exchange of letters, often heated but in the end forgiving. From their first letters until Octave's death, Wilbur and Orville would consider Octave Chanute a valuable asset in the discovery of human flight. Without Chanute's constant respect and encouragement the Wrights, perhaps, would have floundered much longer that they did.

In the end, Wilbur said of Octave, "Mr. Chanute's sympathetic interest in our work was one of the chief stimulants which kept us at work till we attained success. We therefore owe him a great debt of gratitude… Without it we might have quit and thus failed. Mr. Chanute is one of the truest gentlemen we have ever known and a sympathetic friend."[1]

***

[1]*Miracle at Kitty Hawk*, F. Kelly
The Bishop's Boys, Dr. Tom Crouch
The Wright Brothers, A Biography, F. Kelly
Wilbur and Orville: A Biography, F. Howard

Success was not a secret.

"It is a perfect marvel to me that you have kept your performances out of the newspapers so long. With so curious a public as our own, and such appetite for sensation as obtains in the press I felt convinced that some enterprising reporter would discover you some time and make you famous." - Octave Chanute 1905[1]

***

The flights in 1903, 1904, and 1905, first in Kitty Hawk and then in Dayton, were not done in secret. They were witnessed and written about. Yet the world did not *believe* the Wrights had flown until 1908 with Wilbur's public demonstration of the Flyer in LeMans, France.

The Wright Brothers submitted a patent application on March 23, 1903 for the design of their 1902 glider covering the method of controlling the wing tips and rudder for balance and lateral control. The patent process would take a considerable time to complete, having to rewrite and revise it a number of times. After their first submittal was returned for clarification they hired a patent lawyer to help with this process

The original submittal date is used for establishing original dating of patents, so the Wrights did not have to worry about the delay. What they did have to worry about was the discovery of their methods of control after Wilbur's talk to the Western Society of Engineers in the fall of 1901, where he gave a glimpse into the methods of control that would become the basis of the patent. This talk was published in Europe and revisited publicly by their friend Octave Chanute. Many aviation pioneers used this information to make Wright-like machines. Wilbur held back enough information however, to keep them guessing at the Wright's solution.

After the final submittal to the patent offices was in, the boys could fly an airplane in public using the same control methods in the patent. There would be little need to hide their success and they made only small attempts to do so. They would have help with the trials from members of the U.S. Life Saving Station in Kill Devil Hills, south of Kitty Hawk NC, and they would continue their trials and improvements in 1904 and 1905, in view of the few who passed by at Huffman Prairie, a small field outside Dayton, Ohio.

They would try to time the flights at Huffman Prairie so as to avoid the interurban trolley line witnesses as they passed by, but that would be difficult as their flights would grow in duration - approaching 30 minutes per flight. The local farmers tending their fields would have a good view of the boys' success and would surely share that information with their friends and families.

The world would not fully accept the Wrights claim to success until they demonstrated their airplane in the summer of 1908, first in Le Mans, France, and then Fort Myer, Virginia. Even French, British and American government officials would not be given demonstrations, only an opportunity to interview the few witnesses that existed.

Patent number 821.939 for a *Flying Machine*, would be approved on May 22 1906, and would be dated March 23 1903, giving the Wrights what would become the pioneer patent of all of aviation. The technology in this patent would affect all future airplanes flown, even today's modern aircraft. The Wrights' use of wing warp, the twisting of the wing tips to effect lift on one side at a time would be a cornerstone of all aviation. Lifting one side of the craft at a time is a fundamental of balancing a flying machine in the air. The Wrights found a way to do this when so many others failed.

Four years of invention and two years of continued innovation would be forever recognized for what it truly was: the beginning of man's ability to fly. Achieved in December of 1903, and announced the same day, success was never a secret. Yet it would be five years before the world believed it as truth.

***

[1]*Miracle at Kitty Hawk*, F. Kelly
The Bishop's Boys, Dr. Tom Crouch
The Wright Brothers, A Biography, F. Kelly
Wilbur and Orville: A Biography, F. Howard

Monuments

"My brother and I are not very strong believers in monuments..."
     -Wilbur Wright 1911[1]

***

At Kill Devil Hills, four miles south of Kitty Hawk, North Carolina, towers a monument to the Wright Brothers. In sight of that monument stands four stone markers marking the landing points of the first four flights made on December 17th, 1903. These are but some of the monuments honoring first flight and the accomplishments of the Wright Brothers.

France has a monument in LeMans and one in Pau, both in locations where Wilbur, in 1908, demonstrated the airplane for the world. Dayton has one overlooking Huffman Prairie where in 1904 - 1905 the boys perfected their machine for the purpose of selling it. Kitty Hawk has one outside of the home of Wm. Tate where Wilbur stayed in 1900 on his first trip to the Outer Banks. But the most prominent one is at Kill Devil Hills celebrating first flight. All these monuments celebrate the early days of flight and the Wright Brothers success. They honor an accomplishment dreamed of for centuries and seriously pursued for fifty years since Sir George Cayley's early glider flights.

In Orville's heart, one honor towered above all of the above mentioned. This honor was given to him by Henry Ford, the automobile industrialist in Dearborn,

Michigan. Ford approached Orville with the idea to move the Wright home, Orville's birthplace, and the Wright Cycle Shop, the workshop where the airplane was designed and built, to The Edison Institute, Ford's museum, outside Detroit, Michigan. Orville was touched by this request and stated: "I have never had a proposal like this before. It means a great deal."

When told that "Mr. Ford wants to see you and your work adequately recognized. He wants to honor you at Greenfield Village as he has honored Thomas Edison and other great scientists. He wants to preserve your work for posterity", Orville wiped away a tear and said Ford was "the greatest man in America…" and would go on to assist Ford with acquiring the buildings and donating a large collection of artifacts to be housed in both buildings.[2]

It would take two years to accomplish the task of removing these buildings to The Edison Institute and their new location on the grounds of Greenfield Village, a collection of historic buildings honoring the greats of American ingenuity such as Ford, Edison, Webster and Lincoln. The dedication of those two buildings took place on what would have been Wilbur's 71st birthday, April 16th 1938.

In attendance at the dedication were some of the greats of aviation along with the surviving members of Orville's extended family, and a large group of pilots who had flown before the great world war. This group of early pilots formed an organization called *The Early Birds* to gather artifacts of early aviation and collect the stories of the pioneers of flight. Their collection now resides in Ford's museum and tells stories of when flight was new.

After the Early Birds approached Ford with their collection, they discussed the significance of the cycle shop in aviation history. Ford had been denied the first airplane for his museum collection years before but when told the workshop was still standing, he understood that he was able to tell the story of four years of scientific research and engineering experimentation. Four years of hard work that accomplished what had become understood to be impossible to man.

A tall stone monument talks of an event in our history. The home of the first men to fly tells the story of how those men became the individuals that *could* achieve flight when so many could not. It takes a mother and a father, a sister and older brothers; it takes an education and a town to shape those people. It takes a workshop in which to make the machine. It takes the help of a machinist employee and the tools they used. It takes a vocation as bicycle makers to first practice the skills of making. It takes the *telling* of these stories.

All of these stories can best be told while standing in the buildings where all of this took place. Ford knew this, and this was the basis of the creation of his Greenfield Village collection in Dearborn, Michigan.

***

[1]*Miracle at Kitty Hawk*, F. Kelly
The Bishop's Boys, Dr. Tom Crouch
The Wright Brothers, *A Biography*, F. Kelly
Wilbur and Orville: A Biography, F. Howard
[2]The Collections of the Henry Ford, Benson Ford
Research Center

Witnessed, Photographed and Announced.

"It seems to me that this may fairly be said to mark the beginning of successful flight through the air by men unaided by balloons."
- Godfrey Lowell Cabot, December 31, 1903[1]

***

On a cold windy day over the sands of the Outer Banks, four miles south of Kitty Hawk, North Carolina, Orville Wright and his brother Wilbur traded four flights at the controls of the world's first successful heavier than air flying machine. The first flight that day was 120 feet and the last flight was 852 feet. A simple coin flip three days earlier determined who would be first to fly on this day.

In the more than 100 years since that event, the Wrights assertion as the first to fly has been repeatedly challenged. Many claim flight before or question the validity of the flights that day. The evidence of first flight is overwhelming and irrefutable, yet the challenges continue.

It starts four years before that day on May 30, 1899, when Wilbur Wright sits down at his sister's writing desk and pens a letter to the Smithsonian Institute requesting a list of books and pamphlets instructing him on how to build a glider. Within days he received those pamphlets and that list. Later that summer Wilbur would build a box kite to test a theory he had gleaned from his reading.

Gliding experimenters before him had hit a brick wall concerning balance while in the air. In a matter of months Wilbur had solved that brick wall and began planning the building of a glider unlike any other that he had read about. This would be documented in letters to Octave Chanute, one of the authors on that list of books suggested by the Smithsonian Institute in their reply to Wilbur's letter.

The witness of the Wright claim to success would be solidified for the generations to come through the letters written by Wilbur, and later by Orville, to Chanute and others who the Wrights befriended. In Kitty Hawk, over the next four years of experimentation, the physical presences of a handful of men and children, and even a dog named Brownie, would back up those claims. Later, on the day of first flight, Orville and Wilbur would walk into town and send a telegram home to their father telling of first flight.

Within a week of first flight, Wilbur and Orville would discover the one piece of evidence that would live through the ages proving first flight. On December 17th, 1903, John Daniels, a member of the Kill Devil Hills Life Saving Station assisting the Wrights with their experiments, pressed the trigger button on Orville's camera snapping a photograph of the Wright Flyer moments after it lifted off the launch rail on the first attempt that day.

In that photograph can be seen Wilbur's footprints in the sand as he ran along side holding the wing level until Orville was able to take control of this with his hips and their cradle device designed to give lift on each wing, one side at a time. This could only happen if the plane was airborne. Those footprints tell a story of historic proportion, capturing first liftoff of an airplane.

Although the details of that day would grow through exaggeration in the newspaper reports and the announcements shared, the simple fact that flight had occurred could not be denied. Yet it would be five years before the world would celebrate first flight.

In the summer and fall seasons of 1904 and 1905, many people riding the train cars passing by Huffman Prairie would have seen Orville or Wilbur practicing flying. Even a bee keeper, A.I. Root, editor of the *Gleanings in Bee Culture* magazine would publish a description of a flight he witnessed at the end of 1904, at the Huffman Prairie field.

These examples of witness through photos, articles and letters give us a treasure for the ages, telling the true story of early flight. The challenges continue but the evidence is clear. First flight belongs rightly to the Wright Brothers.

***

[1]*Miracle at Kitty Hawk*, F. Kelly
The Bishop's Boys, Dr. Tom Crouch
The Wright Brothers, A Biography, F. Kelly
Wilbur and Orville: A Biography, F. Howard
Hidden Images, L. Tise

74574995R00035

Made in the USA
Middletown, DE
27 May 2018